Bowling Shirts

Joe Tonelli & Marc Luers

4880 Lower Valley Road, Atglen, PA 19310

Copyright © 1998 by Joe Tonelli and Marc Luers
Library of Congress Catalog Card Number: 97-80242

All rights reserved. No part of this work may be reproduced or used in any form or by any means—graphic, electronic, or mechanical, including photocopying or information storage and retrieval systems—without written permission from the copyright holder.

Photography by Joy Shih
Book design by Blair R.C. Loughrey

ISBN: 0-7643-0117-9
Printed in Hong Kong
1 2 3 4

Published by Schiffer Publishing Ltd.
4880 Lower Valley Road
Atglen, PA 19310
Phone: (610) 593-1777; Fax: (610) 593-2002
E-mail: Schifferbk@aol.com
Please write for a free catalog.
This book may be purchased from the publisher.
Please include $3.95 for shipping.

Please try your bookstore first.

We are interested in hearing from authors with book ideas on related subjects.

Dedication

Two Italian wooden figures of woman bowlers, machine-carved, dyed woods with plastic eyes. c. 1950s. $25-$35 each.

To Joe and Donna Tonelli, my collecting friends and parents. Without their love, time and knowledge I may never have become a collector.

And to Kathryn for her time, patience, help and love. Without her I would not have been able to finish this book.

Joe Tonelli

Acknowledgments

Over the years I have met many wonderful people through collecting. I would like to thank all of them for making it a wonderful hobby and business. Special thanks to the following people whom I have had the pleasure of working with in the field of vintage clothing.

Ron Holloway
Reva Young
George and Marge Guzlas
Bob and Megan Morrison
Mike West
Motonobu Sato
Kuniaki Go
Masumi Saito
Shigeru Tanaka

I thank the following people for allowing us to use shirts and items from their collections.
Irving I. Flasher
Todd Hegg and Maribeth Mertes
Gabriela's
Zalkin, Inc.

A bowling alley's wall of champions. *Courtesy of Duke's Bowl, Abbotsford, Wisconsin.*

Contents

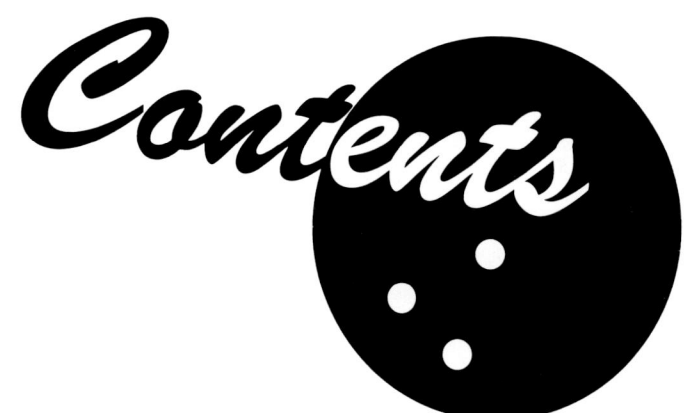

Introduction	7
Aco Design	9
Air-Flo Sportswear	10
Angeltown of California	52
Champion Design in Wisconsin	54
Coast to Coast National Shirt Shop	55
Conqueror Style	56
Coronet	57
Crown Prince	58
Donegal	66
Dunbrooke	69
Dunhill Sportswear	69
Eklund Clothing Company	71
Hilton	72
King Louie	96
Lane Mate	128
MacGregor	129
Marlboro	130
Master Bowler	131
Nat Nast	133
Olympian	140
Richman 300	142
Sea Island	143
Service Bowling Shirt	144
Shapely Classic	149
Shorty Bowlaway	150
Smoky Bowling	151
T. K. Embroidery	152
The Lord Penguin	153
The Strike	154
The Swingster	155
301, Better Than Perfect	156
300 Series	157
Topps	158
Webber Bowling Shirt Company	159

Introduction

    The bowling shirt truly came to life in the 1950s. Although shirts have been around since the early 1930s, the best colors and designs were seen in the 50s. Companies such as *Crown Prince*, *Air-Flo*, *Hilton*, and *Nat-Nast* produced shirts by the thousands. Styles, colors, and designs were limited only by each team's imagination. They reflected a time when people loved their big cars, drive-ins, bowling alleys and flashy clothing. Bowlers wanted to show their team spirit and unity with unique team shirts.

    Almost every team had a sponsor whose name was embroidered on the backs of the shirts. The more elaborate team shirts would have company logos embroidered in full color. Not all shirts were embroidered, however, many quality shirts were simply printed or had iron-on lettering and images. In addition, each team member personalized their shirts with embroidered or printed first and last names as well as award patches. Traditionally, the bowler's first name was embroidered on the front of the shirt, usually over the pocket. The last name was embroidered on the left shoulder area of the back yoke. Each bowler's shirt became a canvas to showcase individuality and creativity.

    The height of bowling shirt production was from the 1950s to the 1960s. In the mid-1960s companies such as *Brunswick* and *AMF*, working with large investors, started building large 20-40 lane bowling alleys with pro shops. They also began producing their own shirts and equipment. This change in shirt production, the introduction of unions to the textile industry, along with a decline of company sponsored teams, forced many small, independent companies out of business.

Double inside seam stitching.

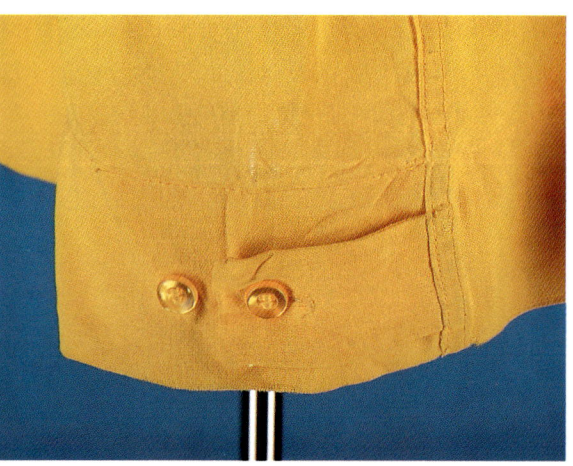

Two button side cinch tab on shirt jac.

Two button cinch on orange shirt jac.

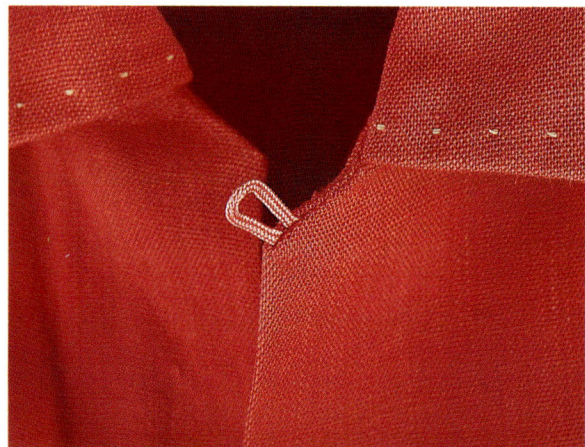

Elastic top button loop on pink shirt.

Fabric top button loop on green shirt.

Unique bowling shirts and small, family-owned alleys have sadly become a thing of the past. Today there are only a few bowling shirt manufacturers left, such as *Hilton*, *King Louie*, and *Brunswick*. Because the cost is so high, very few unique shirts are made. Simple printing is done and the shirts have no embroidery. Shirts can be dated by the fabric, construction of the shirt, embroidery, and printing. Pre-1950s shirts are made of gabardine, have no stitching on the outside seam of the collar, have a button loop at the neck and all designs and lettering were embroidered. In addition, most of the shirts from the 1930s to 1950 were long sleeved versions.

The introduction of predominately short sleeved shirts began in the 1950s. Most 1960s bowling shirts were made from 100% cotton or 100% rayon, and also had a button loop at the neck. These shirts continued to have embroidery but the use of printed and flocked designs and lettering became more common.

In the 1970s, 100% polyester, quarter button front pull-over shirts were made. Most of these shirts had simple printing on them, the days of embroidery were over. From 1980 to the present, shirts have been made from a 50/50 blend of polyester and cotton. Most of these shirts have only simple printing or were not printed at all.

Aco Design

Label: Aco Design, Brewster, charcoal gray, two front button patch pockets, straight bottom hem. Back has two pleated side vents and direct embroidery stitching. Rayon. c. 1950s. $35-$50.

9

Air-Flo Sportswear

Irving Flasher honored at a State of Minnesota Bowling Awards Dinner, c. 1950s.

The *Air-flo Sportswear Company* was started in 1950 by Irving I. Flasher, and was located in Minneapolis, Minnesota. The *Air-flo* name came from Mr. Flasher's unique shirt design that had special vents under each arm allowing air to flow through. Another characteristic feature of these shirts was their special flocked lettering with sparkles. The most unique feature, however, were the patented bowling pin buttons that came in three colors: red, white and black.

In the 1950s *Air-flo* shirts sold for $5.95 for the long sleeve version, and $4.95 for short sleeve. For $2.00 extra, an unlimited number of embroidered or flocked letters could be applied. There was a 25¢ fee for adding a name and a $1.00 one-time set-up charge for company logos. Today some of these same shirts can sell for over $250.00 each.

Air-flo Sportswear was a sponsor of the 1950s television show "Bowlerama", Junior League Bowlers, and American Bowling Congress Championship Teams and Tournaments. The company closed in 1969, ending the production of one of the finest bowling shirts ever made.

Irving Flasher, retired designer and owner of *Air-flo Sportswear Company*.

Plaque recognizing *Air-flo*'s sponsorship of the American Bowling Congress.

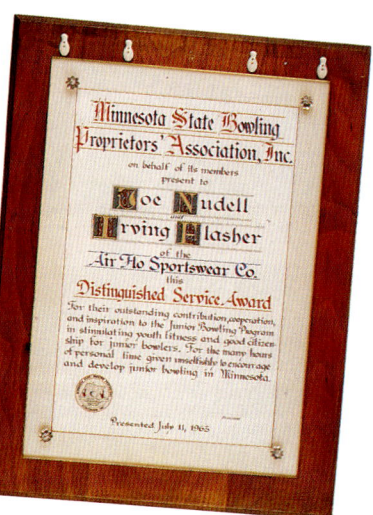

Award plaque given to *Air-flo Sportswear Company*.

Label: *Air-flo*, green, top button loop, signature bowling pin buttons, one patch pocket, direct embroidery on back. Rayon. c. 1960s. $45-$65.

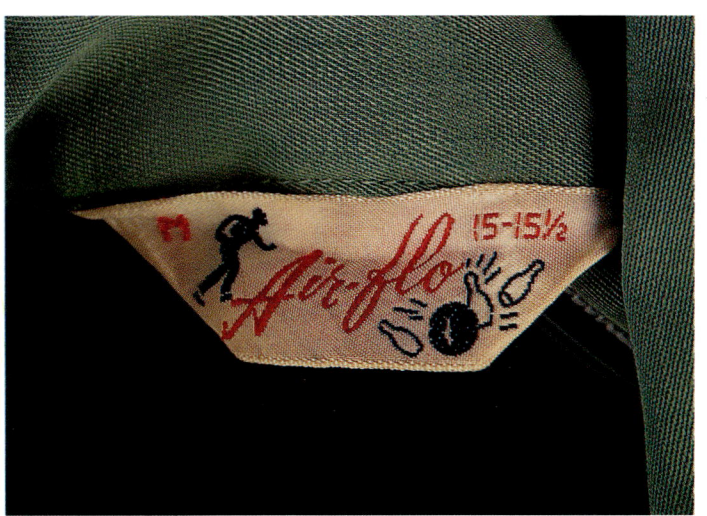

Label: *Air-flo*, brown, top button loop, two front flap patch pockets, straight side vented hem, signature bowling pin buttons with extra button on bottom, direct embroidery back design. Rayon. c. 1960s. $75-$100.

Collar top stitching detail.

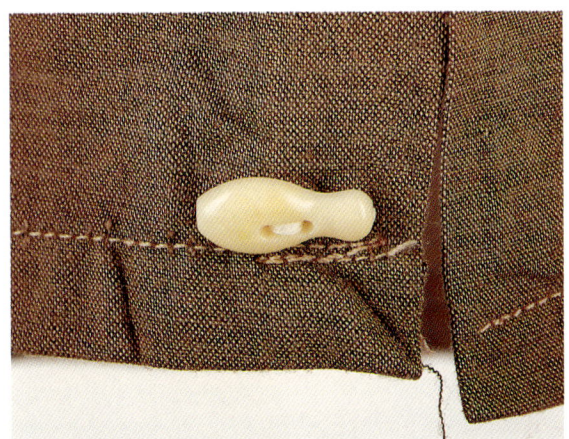

Air-flo shirts featured their signature bowling pin buttons and an extra button on the bottom of the shirt.

13

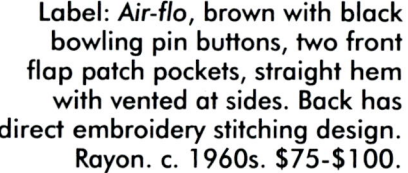

Label: *Air-flo*, brown with black bowling pin buttons, two front flap patch pockets, straight hem with vented at sides. Back has direct embroidery stitching design. Rayon. c. 1960s. $75-$100.

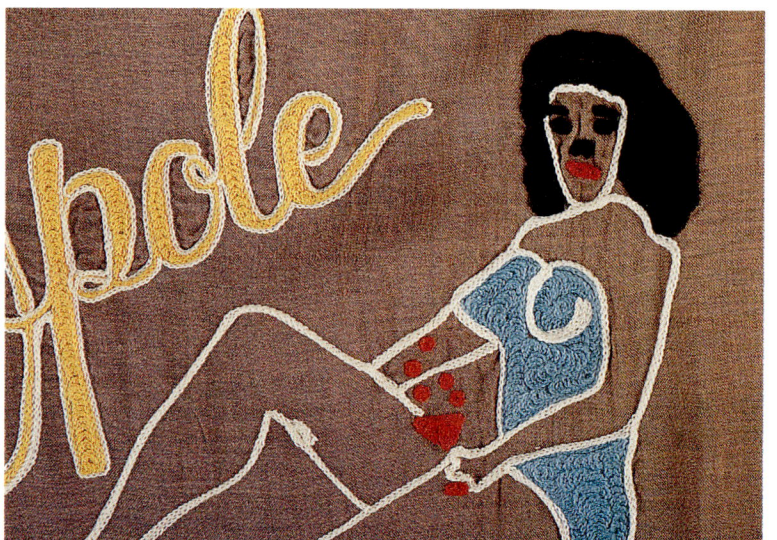

Label: *Air-flo*, light denim blue, with signature black bowling pin buttons, elastic loop top button, two button patch pockets, straight hem with side vents. Back has red direct embroidery outlined in yellow. Spun rayon. c. 1960s. $45-$65.

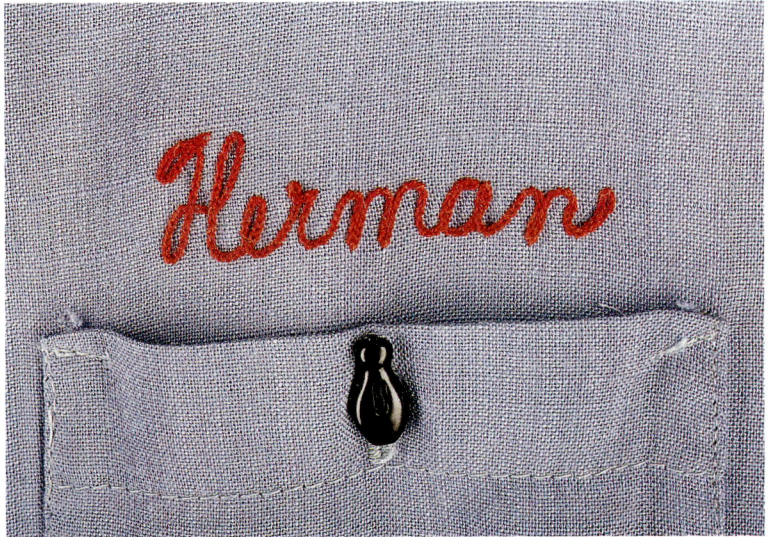

Label: *Air-flo*, red shirt jac with black and white zebra stripe trim at arms, one front button pocket with placket trim. Flocked printed back design and name over front pocket. This Air-flo shirt does not have the signature bowling pin buttons. Rayon. c. 1950s. $65-$85.

Label: *Air-flo*, white with contrasting black trim on front patch pocket, black pleated tabs on sleeves, black undercollar trim, black signature bowling pin buttons with extra button on bottom front hem, straight bottom hem. Back has contrasting black vents to the waist, and flocked printed design. Rayon. c. 1960s. $35-$50.

Label: *Air-flo*, red with signature bowling pin buttons, contrasting white pleated vents on short sleeves and back, white band trim on front patch pocket, white undercollar trim. Black sparkling flocked print name and back design. Rayon, c. 1960s. $35–$50.

Contrasting pleated vent on short sleeve.

Label: *Air-flo*, yellow with two front button patch pockets, black signature bowling pin buttons, straight bottom hem. The name in blue block lettering is unusual. Back has direct embroidery stitching. Spun rayon. c. 1960s. $35-$50.

Label: *Air-flo*, red with one patch pocket, contrasting white undercollar trim, novelty "strikes" knit trim on sleeves and on back of arms, signature bowling pin buttons. Sparkling flocked printing on back. Rayon. c. 1960s. $45-$65.

Label: *Air-flo*, black, white signature bowling pin buttons with extra button at bottom front hem, one button patch pocket, straight bottom hem. Direct embroidery stitching on back. Rayon, c. 1960s. $45-$65.

Label: *Air-flo*, white with contrasting black pleated vent tabs on sleeves, black signature bowling pin buttons with extra button on bottom front, black trim on inside front chest pocket, looped button fastener at neck, straight bottom hem. Back features contrasting side vents to the waist, and flocked printing. Rayon. c. 1960s. $50-$75.

Label: *Air-flo*, deep red, long sleeves with adjustable two button cuffs, contrasting yellow piping down the sleeves, yellow undercollar trim, two patched flap pockets, straight bottom hem. Back has pleated side vents, and direct embroidery stitching. Rayon. c. 1950s. $75-$100.

Label: *Air-flo*, cobalt blue, one button patch pocket, signature white bowling pin buttons with extra button at bottom front, straight bottom hem. Direct embroidery back design. Rayon. c. 1960. $50-$75.

Label: *Air-flo*, deep red, contrasting black collar with red trim, signature black bowling pin buttons, black trim on patch pocket, decorative tabs on sleeves, straight bottom hem. Flocked printing design. Rayon. c. 1960s. $100-$125.

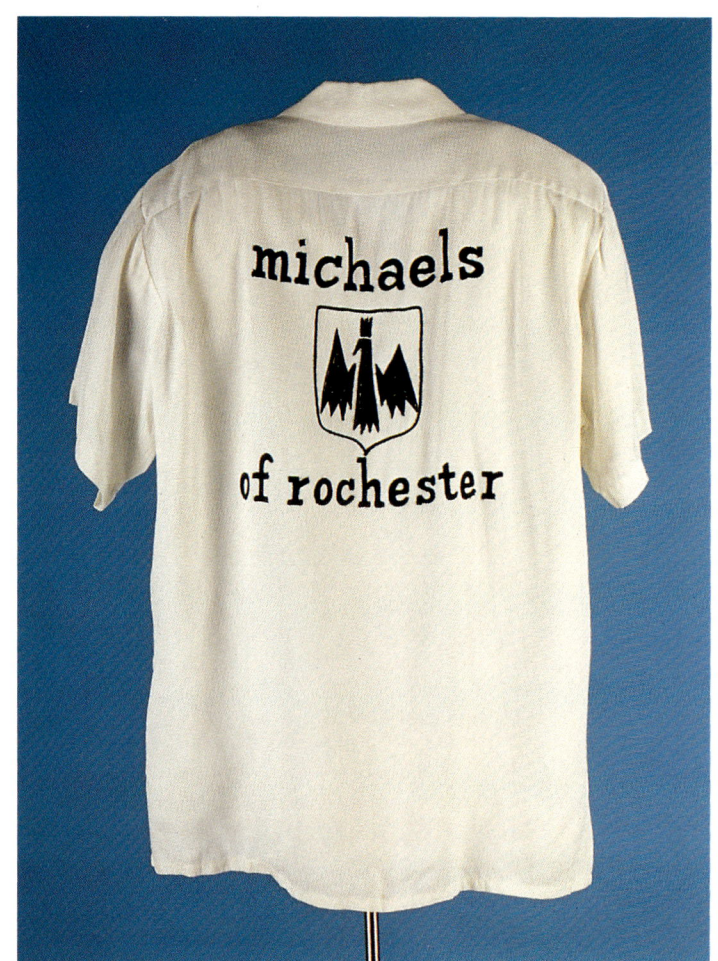

Label: *Air-flo*, white with one button patch pocket, black signature bowling pin buttons with extra button, straight bottom hem. Direct embroidery design on back. Rayon. c. 1960s. $45-$60.

Label: *Air-flo*, golden yellow, one front button patch pocket, black signature bowling pin buttons with extra button at bottom fron, straight bottom hem. Back of shirt has velour flocked printing. Rayon. c. 1960. $45-$60.

Leather bowling shoes, c. 1970s.

Label: *Air-flo*, red, signature bowling pin buttons with extra button at front hem, two button patch pockets, straight bottom hem. Back has gathered pleated shoulder panel and direct embroidery design. Rayon. c. 1960. $50-$65.

Label: *Air-flo*, black, contrasting white undercollar trim, novelty "strikes" knit trim on sleeves, signature white bowling pin buttons with extra button at bottom front, straight bottom hem. Back has direct embroidery stitching. Rayon. c. 1960s. $60-$75.

Label: *Air-flo*, aqua, top stitching on collar, signature bowling pin buttons, two button patch pockets, straight bottom hem with side vents. Applique felt lettering on back. Spun rayon. c. 1960s. $45-$60.

Label: *Air-flo*, red with contrasting white undercollar trim, white piping down the sleeves, white signature bowling pin buttons, straight hem with side vents. Back has sparkling flocked printing. Combed cotton. c. 1960s. $50-$75.

Label: *Air-flo*, navy blue, signature bowling pin buttons with extra button at front hem, one button patch pocket, straight bottom hem. Back has direct embroidery stitching. Rayon. c. 1960s. $45-$65.

Brass bowler on wooden base, 1958.

Label: *Air-flo*, white with contrasting black and white novelty "strikes" trim on collar, sleeves and back of arms, black signature bowling pin buttons with extra button on bottom front, one button patch pocket, straight bottom hem. Direct embroidery stitching. Rayon. c. 1950s. $100-$125.

Label: *Air-flo*, red, one button patch pocket, contrasting white undercollar trim, novelty "strikes" knit trim on arms and sleeve hem, signature white bowling pin buttons, straight bottom hem. Back has direct embroidery stitching. Rayon. c. 1960s. $50-$75.

Label: *Air-flo*, golden yellow, black signature bowling pin buttons, one button patch pocket, straight bottom hem. Back has flock print design. Clarence's shirt sports two patches sewn onto the sleeves. Two shirts from the same team is considered a rare find. Rayon. c. 1960s. $45-$65 each.

Label: *Air-flo*, red with signature white bowling pin buttons, two front button patch pockets, straight bottom hem. Back has gathered pleated panel and direct embroidery stitching. Note that the middle button on the front of the shirt was replaced with a round one and the two pocket buttons are lost. Rayon. c. 1960s. $35-$45.

Label: *Air-flo*, black with white signature bowling pin buttons, one button patch pocket, straight bottom hem. Direct embroidery stitching on back. Rayon. c. 1960s. $45-$65.

Label: *Air-flo*, white with one button patch pocket, black signature bowling pin buttons with extra button at bottom front, straight bottom hem. Back has direct embroidery stitching. Spun rayon. c. 1960s. $40-$50.

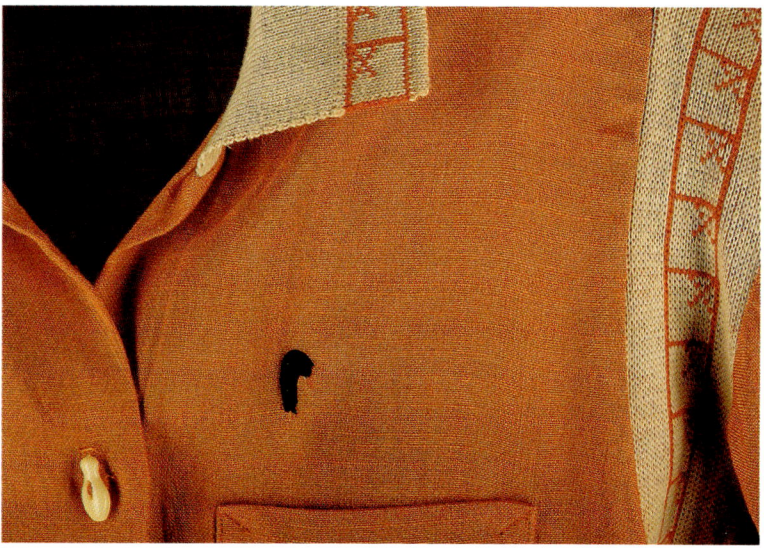

Label: *Air-flo*, orange woman's tapered shirt, cream colored novelty "strikes" design knit collar and shoulder trim, one patch pocket, straight bottom hem. Flocked printed name over front pocket has missing letters. Back has sparkle flocked printed design and lettering. Spun rayon. c. 1950s. $75-$95.

Label: *Air-flo*, white with one button patch pocket, black signature bowling pin buttons with extra button at bottom front, straight bottom hem. Back has direct embroidery stitching. Rayon. c. 1960s. $40-$50.

Label: *Air-flo*, red, white signature bowling pin buttons with extra button at bottom front hem, one button patch pocket, straight bottom hem. Back has sparkle flocked printing with missing letters that spells out Clarence's Tavern Eden. Rayon. c. 1960s. $40-$50.

Label: *Air-flo*, black with contrasting white piping down length of sleeves, white undercollar trim, two button patch pockets, signature bowling pin buttons. Back has direct embroidery design. Rayon. c. 1960s. $45-$65.

Label: *Air-flo*, red, white signature bowling pin buttons with extra button at front bottom hem, one button patch pocket, straight bottom hem. Back has pleated side vents and flocked printed design. Garbardine. c. 1960s. $65-$85.

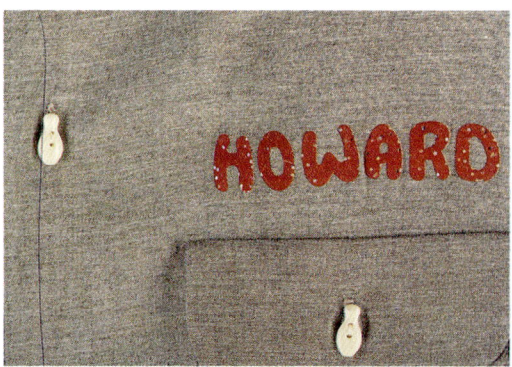

Label: *Air-flo*, gray, two button flap patch pockets, signature white bowling pin buttons with extra button at bottom front hem, top stitch collar, straight bottom hem with vented sides. Back has sparkle flocked printing. Combed cotton. c. 1960. $65-$85.

Label: *Air-flo*, cadet blue, two front button patch pockets, signature white bowling buttons, straight bottom hem with vented sides. Stitched design over front left pocket. Back has sparkle flocked printing design. Spun rayon. c. 1960s. $100-$125.

Label: *Air-flo*, white with contrasting black trim on patch pocket, tabs on sleeves, undercollar trim, and signature bowling pin buttons, straight bottom hem. Back of shirt has contrasting black pleated vents to the waist, and direct embroidery. Rayon. c. 1960s. $45-$65.

Label: *Air-flo*, black, white signature bowling pin buttons, one button patch pockets, straight bottom hem. Direct embroidery stitching on back. This shirt does not have a name on the front. Rayon. c. 1960s. $45-$65.

Chrome mini-bars with liquor dispensers and shot glasses, one with a bowler on cover; the other has pins and a ball, on black enamel steel pedestals. c. 1950s or 60s. $40-$60.

Label: *Air-flo*, bright green, white signature bowling pin buttons, long sleeves with adjustable cuffs, straight bottom hem. Back has direct embroidery stitching. Note that the front buttons are misaligned, indicating that they have been replaced. Rayon. c. 1950s. $75-$90.

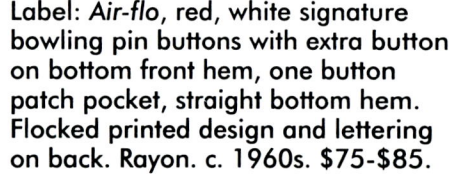

Label: *Air-flo*, red, white signature bowling pin buttons with extra button on bottom front hem, one button patch pocket, straight bottom hem. Flocked printed design and lettering on back. Rayon. c. 1960s. $75-$85.

Label: *Air-flo*, black, with contrasting white piping down the length of each sleeve, white signature bowling pin buttons with extra button at bottom front hem, straight bottom hem. Direct embroidery stitching on back. Rayon. c. 1960s. $65-$75.

Label: *Air-flo*, light blue, contrasting red collar with blue trim, red tabs on sleeves, red trim on patch pocket, signature red bowling pin buttons, straight bottom hem. The red buttons are very rare. Red direct embroidery stitching on back. Rayon. c. 1960s. $50-$60.

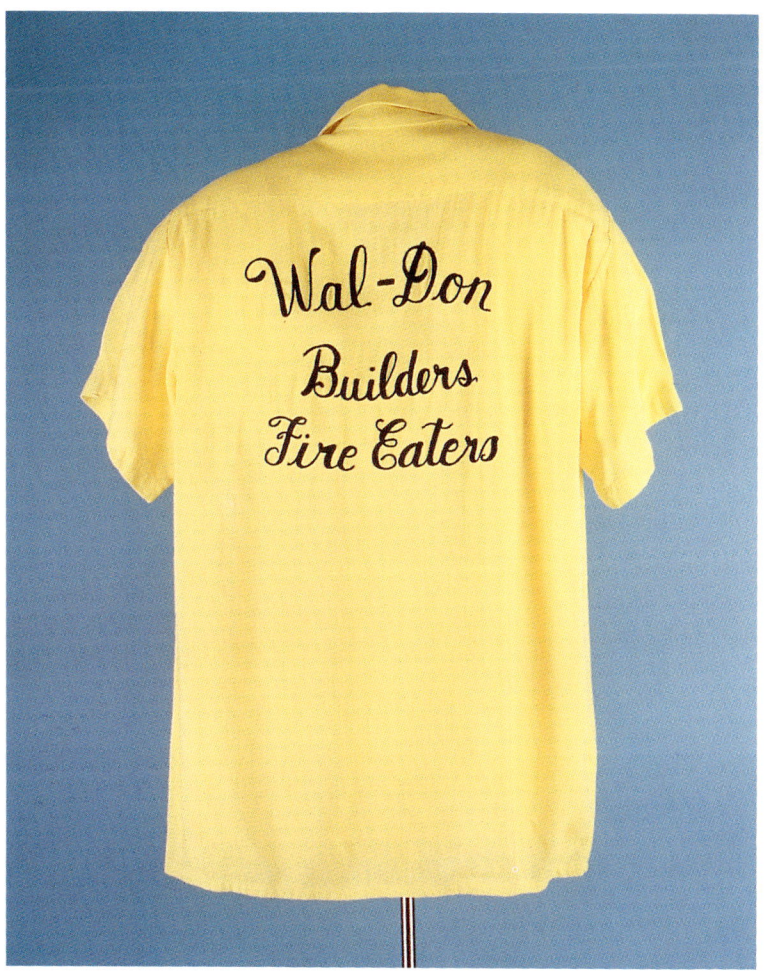

Label: *Air-flo*, yellow, one button patch pocket, black signature bowling pin buttons, straight bottom hem. Direct embroidery stitching. Spun rayon. c. 1960s. $45-$55.

Label: *Air-flo*, dark pink, two front patch pockets with flaps, point stitching on collar and on pocket flaps, elastic loop for top button, straight bottom hem. Direct embroidery stitching on back, and on sleeve shoulder. This shirt does not have the signature bowling pin buttons. Spun rayon. c. 1960s. $65-$85.

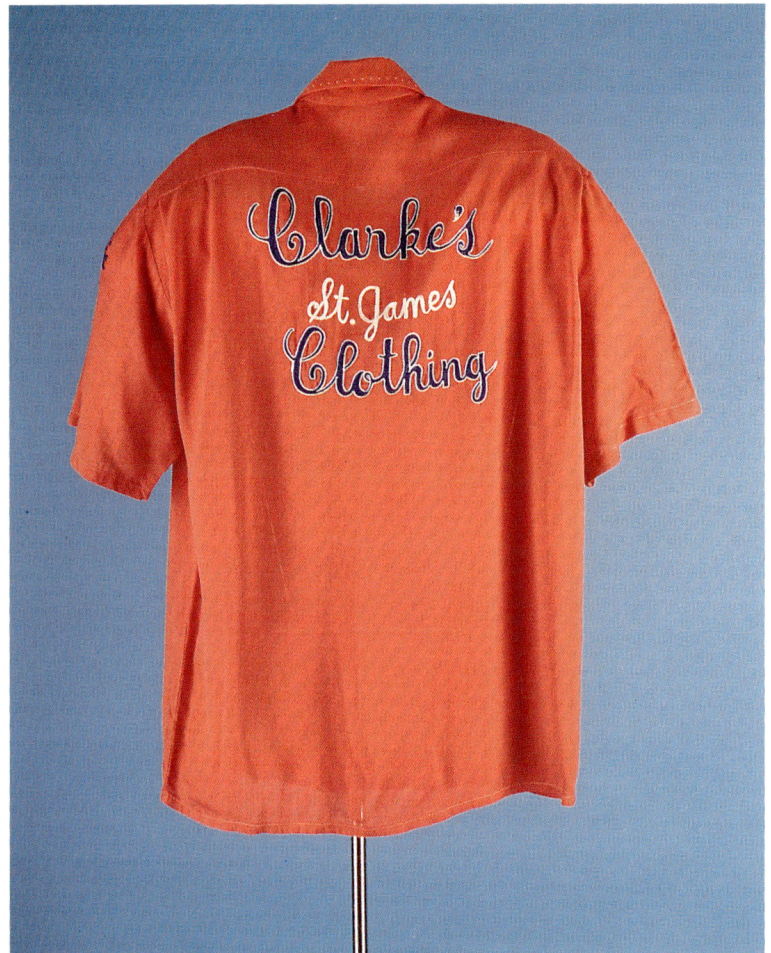

Label: *Air-flo*, white, two front button patch pockets, black signature bowling pin buttons with extra button, straight bottom hem with side vents. Back has sparkle flocked print design. Spun rayon. c. 1960s. $50-$60.

 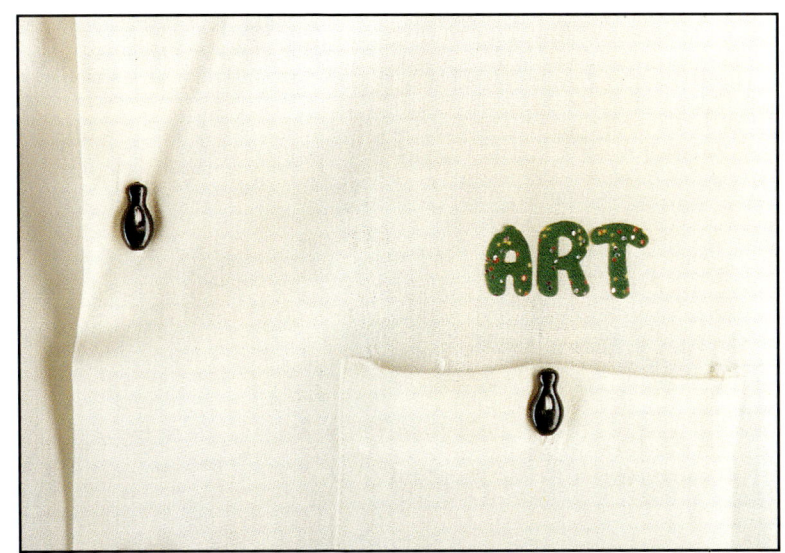

Angeltown Of California

Label: *Angeltown of California*, mustard gold shirt jac with open rounded collar, one patch pocket. Direct embroidery stitching. Rayon/acetate/combed cotton blend. c. 1960s. $40-$50.

Label: *Angeltown*, white, two button patch pockets, straight bottom hem. Back has direct embroidery stitching. Rayon. c. 1960s. $25-$30.

Champion Design In Wisconsin

Label: *Champion Design in Wisconsin*, forest green, pointed collars, two patch pockets, straight bottom hem. Direct embroidery stitching design on back. Rayon. c. 1940s. $50-$60.

Coast To Coast National Shirt Shop

Label: *Coast to Coast National Shirt Shop Garbardine*, rust, long sleeves with adjustable button cuffs, two front flap patch pockets with center folded pleats, straight hem. Back has direct embroidery design. Note that a matching fabric patch has been sewn over an original name. Gabardine. c. 1940s. $50-$60.

Conqueror Style

Label: *Conqueror Style*, light blue service work shirt, shirttail hem, two front patch pockets with pen slot on left pocket, direct embroidery back design. Cotton. c. 1950s. $50–$60.

Coronet

Label: *Coronet*, dark tan, two patch flap pockets, two-tone green direct embroidery on back, green embroidery on sleeve and pocket flap, straight bottom hem. Gabardine. c. 1930s. $75-$100.

Crown Prince

Label: *Crown Prince*, woman's olive green shirt jac, one button patch chest pocket with eagle patch, vented short sleeves, embroidered back design. Rayon. c. 1960s. $35-$45.

Label: *Crown Prince*, woman's red shirt tapered in front, contrasting white trim on collar, white piping on sleeves and front patch pocket. Woman bowler design embroidered on front pocket. Direct embroidery back design. Rayon. c. 1960s. $25-$35.

Label: *Crown Prince*, black, long sleeves with button cuffs, two patch pockets with domed (rounded top) flaps. Back has colorful direct embroidery stitching design. Gabardine. c. 1940s. $100-$125.

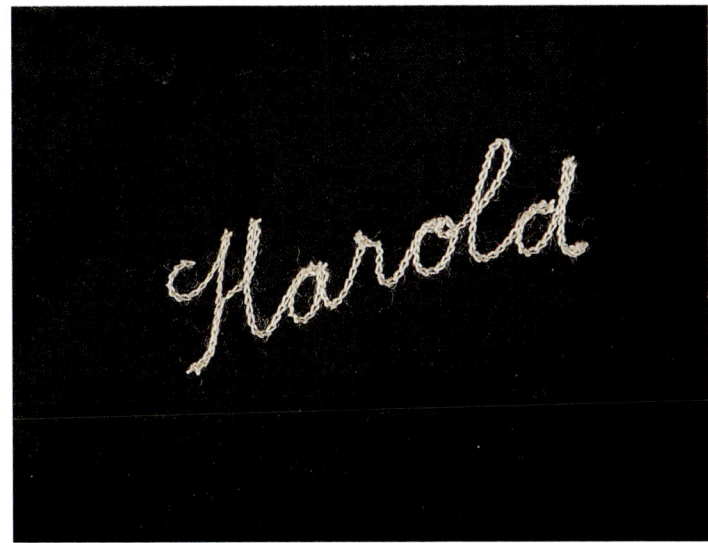

Label: *Crown Prince*, light aqua, long sleeves with adjustable button cuffs, white satin inner yoke interfacing, two patch pockets with center folded pleats and flaps, shirttail hem. Back has direct embroidery stitching. Rayon. c. 1940s. $60-$70.

Hand tooled leather bowling bag with space on the bottom for shoes. c. 1950's. $30-$40.

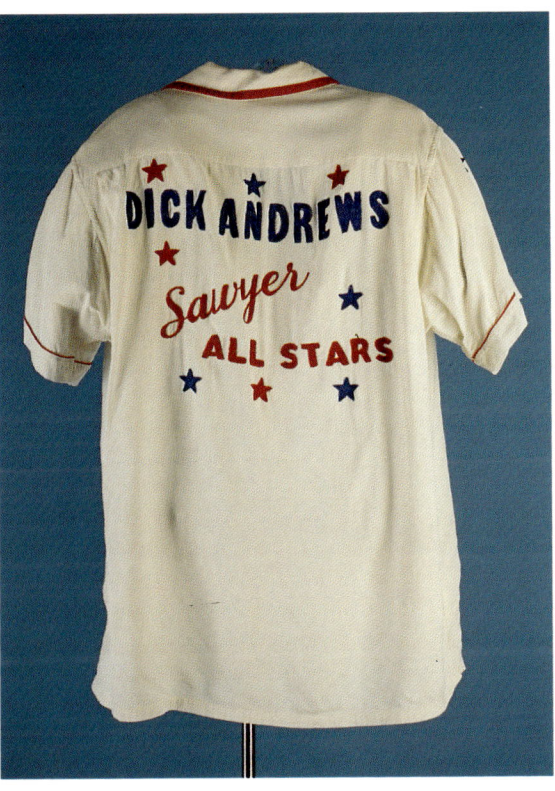

Label: *Crown Prince*, white with contrasting red trim on collar, pockets and sleeves, two patch pockets, straight bottom hem. Front pocket features an embroidered male bowler image. Back and sleeves have direct embroidered stars and lettering. Rayon. c. 1960. $75-$95.

Label: *Crown Prince*, butter yellow, long sleeves with adjustable cuffs, two front button pockets with flaps and center pleats, straight bottom hem. Rayon. c. 1940s. $75-$95.

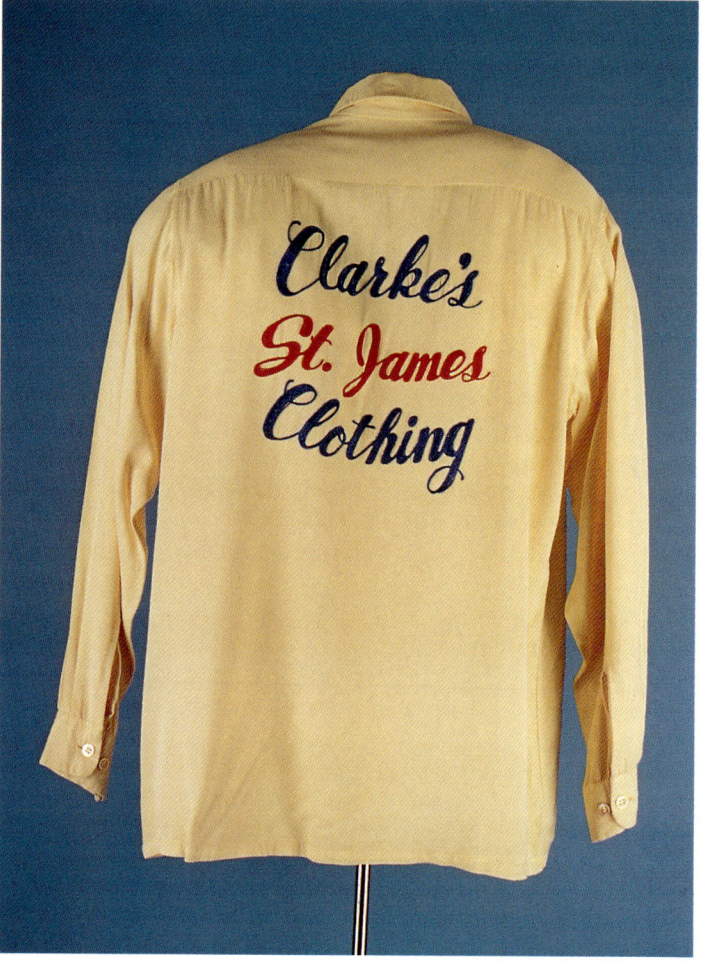

Label: *Crown Prince*, white with black and white gingham check trim on collar and on patch pocket, straight bottom hem. Velour flocked printing on back. Rayon. c. 1960s. $25-$35.

Donegal

Label: *Donegal Fitzhugh*, blue, two patch pockets, straight bottom hem. Back has direct embroidery stitching. Rayon. c. 1950s. $35–$50.

Dunbrooke

Label: *Dunbrooke*, sapphire blue shirt jac, one patch pocket, raglan sleeves with knit stripe trim, notched sleeves. Direct embroidery design on back. Rayon. c. 1960. $50-$60.

Label: *Dunbrooke*, white with two button patch pockets, shirttail hem. Direct embroidery name, flock printing on back. Rayon. c. 1960. $25-$35.

Dunhill Sportswear

Label: *Dunhill Sportswear*, red, two front flap pockets, long sleeves with adjustable cuffs, direct embroidery back design. Gabardine. c. 1940s. $75-$95.

Label: *Dunhill*, white, contrasting green collar and trim on two patch pockets, shirttail hem. Direct embroidered name over front pocket. Back has printed design. Rayon. c. 1960s. $30-$40.

Eklund Clothing Company

Label: *Eklund Clothing Co., Made by Westmoor, Minneapolis, Land of 10,000 Lakes*, navy blue, satin interior yoke interfacing, two front button flap pockets, shirttail hem. Direct embroidery back design featuring an Indian head. Rayon. c. 1950s. $100-$125.

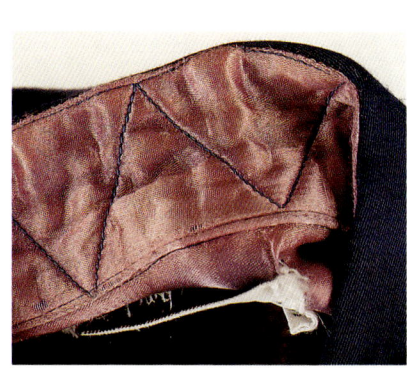

Hilton

Detail of *Hilton* sign. $75-$100.

Hilton shirt rack for store display with Hilton shirts from 1930s to 1960s.

Label: *Hilton*, black, two patched pockets with center pocket pleats, shirttail hem, direct embroidery with red outline. Rayon. c. 1960s. $65-$75.

Label: *Hilton*, red with blue and white ribbed knit trim at arms, blue and white stitched trim on sleeves. Stitched name on front and back yoke at shoulder, embroidered pin and crown design on front pocket. Printed back design. Cotton. c. late 1960s. $30-$40.

Label: *Hilton*, woman's black shirt jac with side button cinch at waist, open v-neck collar, elbow length sleeves, lower patch pocket with stitched name and novelty embroidery. Back design has naugahide applique. Rayon. c. 1960. $30-$40.

Label: *Hilton*, wedgewood blue shirt jac, front pocket with fold-over flap and embroidered pin and crown design, two shoulder patches. Direct embroidery stitching on back. Rayon. c. 1960s. $60-$70.

Label: *Hilton*, black shirt jac with adjustable button waist cinch, front pocket with embroidered bowling pin with crown design. Back has flocked printing. Rayon. c. 1960s. $50-$60.

Label: *Hilton*, pea green with black and white ribbed trim at arms and sleeves, one patch pocket with embroidered pin and crown, straight hem. Back design and front name has flocked print. Cotton, c. 1960s. $30-$40.

Label: *Hilton*, red, two button front pleated pockets, double stitching on collars, shirttail hem. Back has applique fabric design. Rayon. c. 1960s. $40-$50.

Label: *Hilton*, black, two front button pleated patch pockets, stitching accented with satin ribbons, straight bottom hem. Back has a stunning direct embroidery design accented with ribbons. Rayon. c. 1960s. $200-$250.

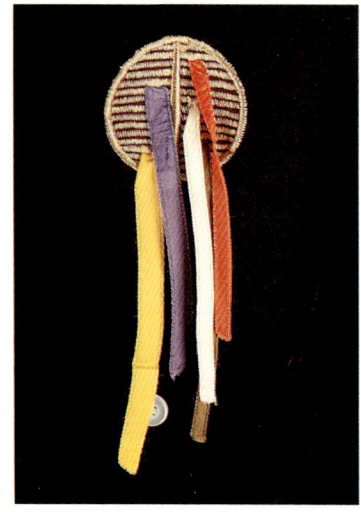

Label: *Hilton*, white with contrasting black collar, black piping trim on sleeves and two front patch pockets, straight bottom hem. Back features contrasting black pleated side vents tapered at waist, and embroidered patch lettering. Rayon. c. 1960s. $35-$45.

Detail of black pleated side vents.

Label: *Hilton*, yellow shirt jac, contrasting black piping trim on sleeves, pocket and at waist hem, black buttons. Back features a logo patch and flocked print lettering. Rayon. c. 1960s. $35-$45.

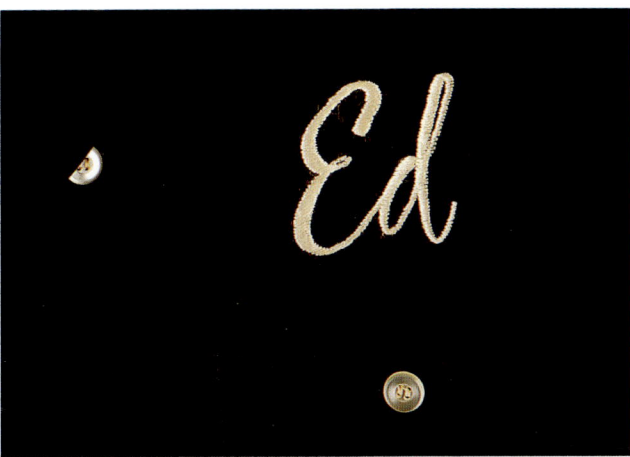

Label: *Hilton*, black, two front pleated button patch pockets, two sleeve patches, shirttail hem. Direct embroidery stitching design on back and on name over front pocket. Rayon. c. 1960s. $50-$70.

83

Label: *Hilton*, kelly green, two button pleated patch pockets, long sleeves with adjustable button cuffs, shirttail hem. Back has flocked printing. Rayon. c. 1950s. $40-$50.

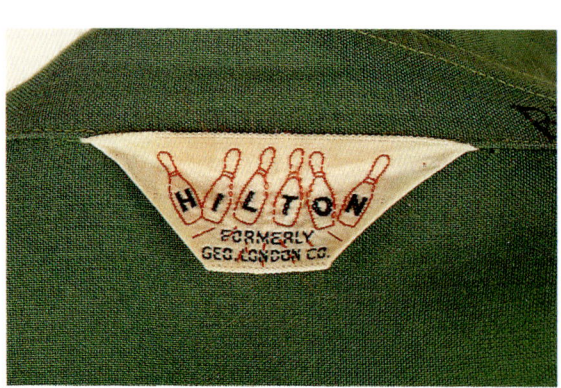

Two Bakelite mini-bars with bowler figures on top, each on black enamel steel pedestal. c. 1950s. $40-$50 each.

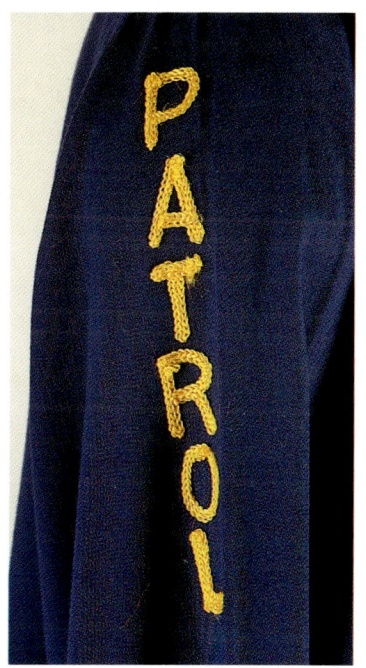

Label: *Hilton*, military blue, long sleeves with adjustable cuffs, two button patch pockets with center folded pleats, shirttail hem. This highly decorated shirt has an embroidered shield patch over the left front pocket, direct embroidery design on back, and direct embroidery lettering down each sleeve. Gabardine. c. 1950s. $75-$100.

85

Label: *Hilton*, white with contrasting red collar, decorative red piping on sleeves and two front patch pockets, straight bottom hem. Back has contrasting red side vents tapered at waist, and flocked printing. Rayon. c. 1960s. $45-$55.

League champions, c. 1950s. *Courtesy of Duke's Bowl, Abbotsford, Wisconsin.*

Label: *Hilton*, woman's light aqua golf and bowling shirt, with open collar, roll up sleeves with button tabs, double buttons on front, lower hip patch pocket, straight bottom hem with side vents. Front pocket and left sleeve feature an embroidered patch. Back has flocked printed design. Combed cotton. c. 1960s. $35-$45.

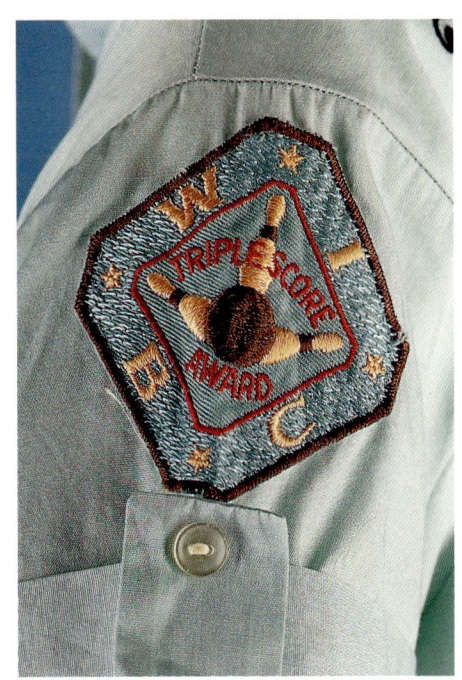

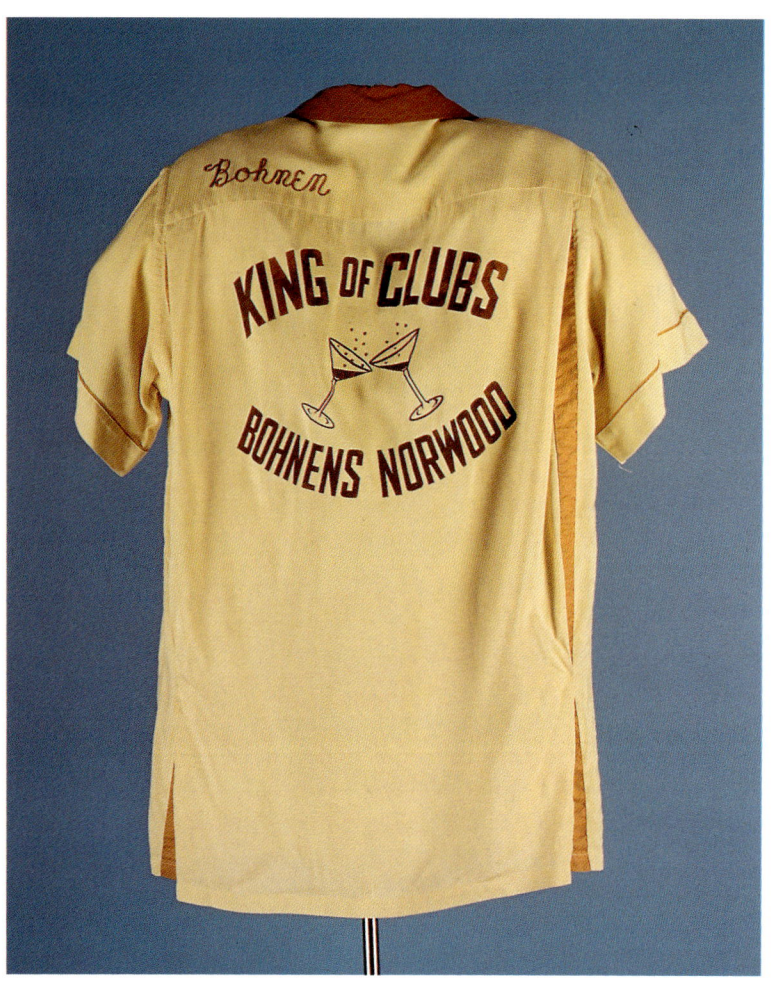

Label: *Hilton*, creamy beige shirt with contrasting brown collar, brown trim on sleeves and patch pockets, straight bottom hem. Back has pleated side vents, and flocked printing. Rayon. c. 1960s. $45-$55.

Label: *Hilton*, woman's white shirt with contrasting red open shawl collar, red trim on sleeves and patch pocket, tapered in front and back at waist, straight bottom hem. Back has contrasting red pleated vent tapered at the waist, and flocked printed letters. Rayon. c. 1960s. $45-$55.

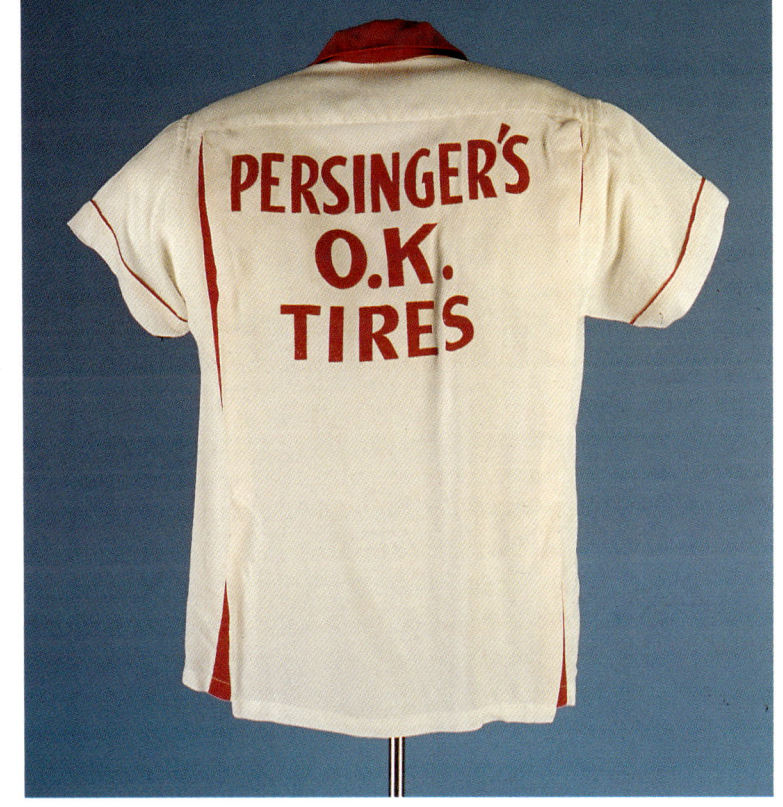

Bowling trophy with metal gilt male bowler and eagles on marble base, 1960-61.

Label: *Hilton*, golden yellow, two front button patch pockets with center folded pleats, shirttail hem. Back has direct straight embroidery. Rayon. c. 1960s. $35-$45.

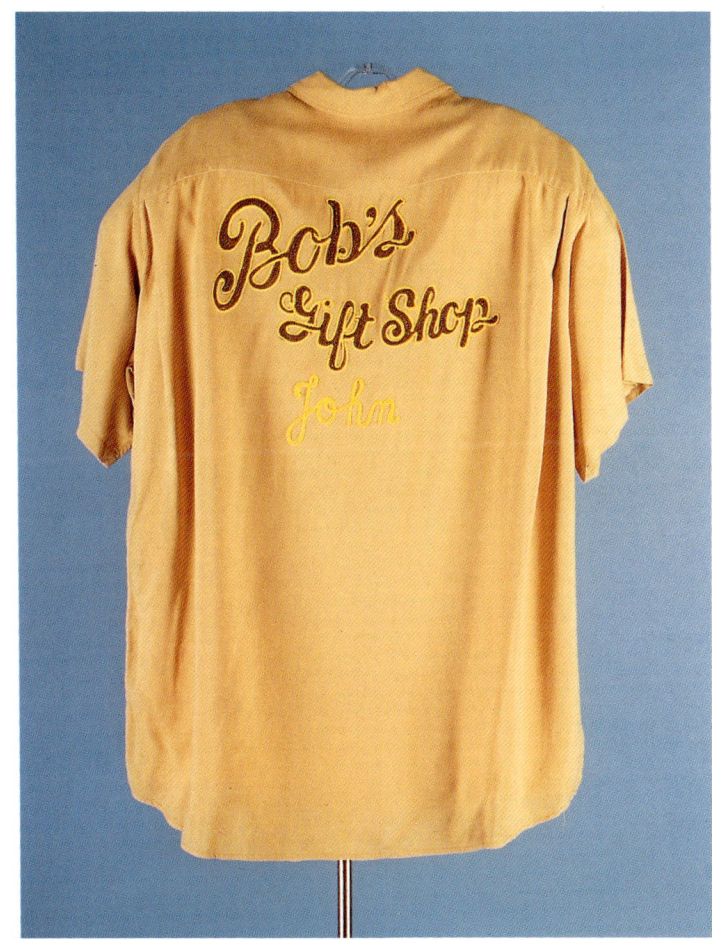

Label: *Hilton*, beige tan, two front button patch pockets with center folded pleats, straight bottom hem. Dark brown direct embroidery outlined in golden yellow. Rayon. c. 1950s. $70-$80.

"Norshore Fuel Oil" sequin patch for bowler's shirt and manufacturer's card of novelty plastic bowling pins and ball shirt buttons. c. 1950s. Patch $10-$20, Buttons $5.

Label: *Hilton*, blue shirt jac, contrasting white piping trim on sleeves, two patch pockets, and hem, contrasting white buttons. Back has contrasting white pleated vents tapered to the waist, and direct embroidery. Permanent Press. c. 1960s. $20-$30.

Label: *Hilton*, red shirt jac, with contrasting black buttons, black piping trim on sleeves, two patch pockets, and hem. Back has flocked printing. Permanent Press. c. 1960s. $20-$30.

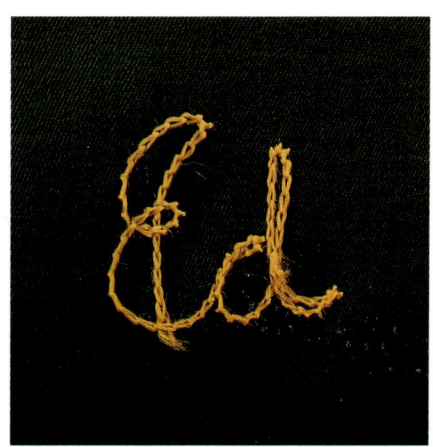
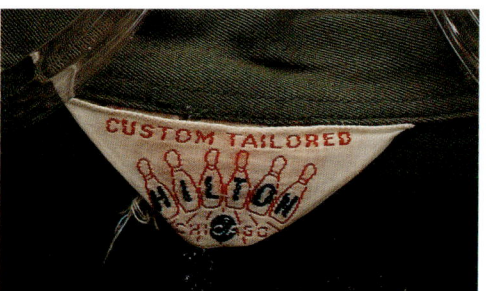

Label: *Hilton*, hunter green, two button patch pockets, straight bottom hem. Back with direct embroidery stitching and a large Texaco logo patch in the center. Rayon. c. 1950s. $75-$95.

Label: *Hilton*, white with contrasting red and white knit trim around arms, and on sleeves, one patch pocket with pin and crown embroidery, straight bottom hem. Back has direct embroidery stitching. Rayon. c. 1960s. $30-$40.

Label: *Hilton*, two-tone green shirt jac with the look of a two-piece, one inside pocket trimmed in darker green to match collar. Direct embroidery stitching over front pocket and on back of shirt. Cotton. c. 1960s. $25-$35.

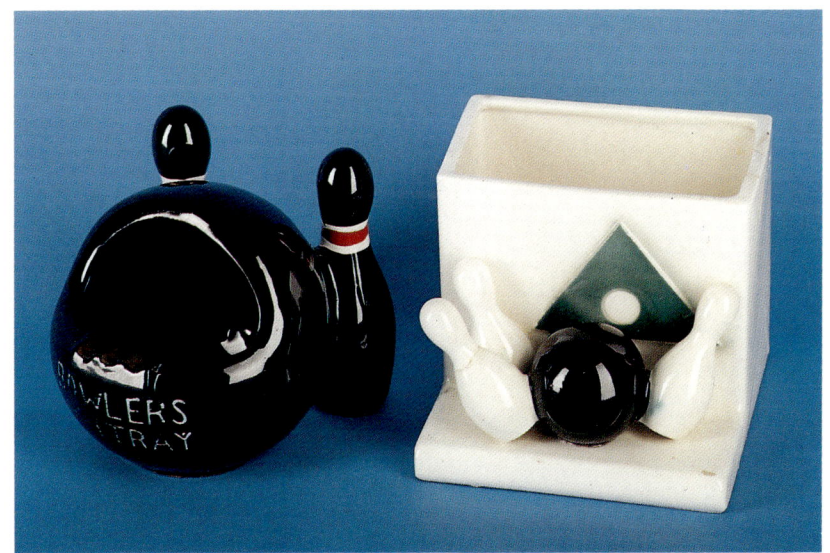

Ceramic bowler ash tray and bowler planter. c. 1960s. $5-$10.

King Louie

Label: *King Louie by Holiday*, green, two front button flap pockets, long sleeves with adjustable cuffs, shirttail hem. Back has pleated side vents tapered at waist, direct embroidery stitching. Rayon. c. 1950s. &75-$95.

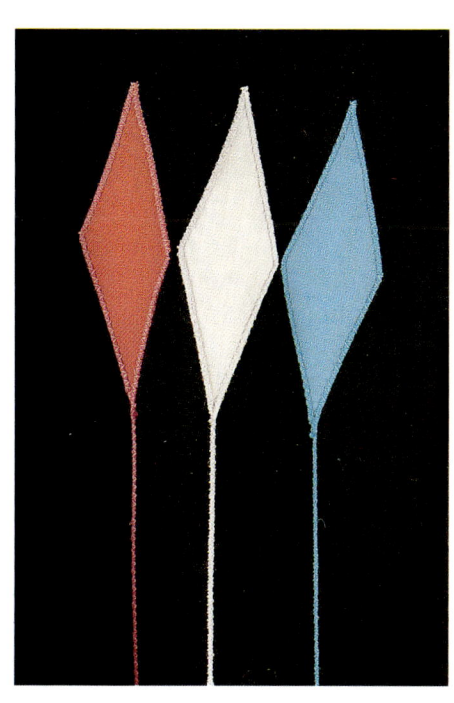

Label: *King Louie by Holiday*, black shirt jac, one patch pocket, three applique diamonds and embroidered stripes on front. Direct embroidery stitching on back. Rayon. c. 1960s. $70-$80.

Label: *King Louie by Holiday*, red shirt jac, one patch pocket in front, applique diamonds and stripes design on front, short sleeves with top stitched hem. Back has flocked print design. Rayon. c. 1960s. $60-$70.

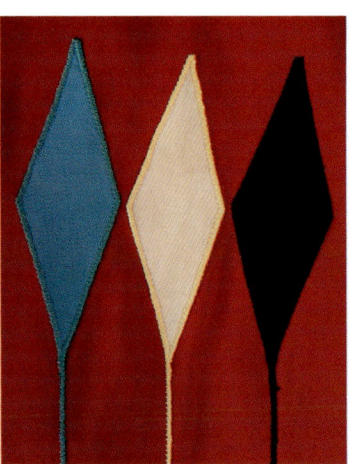

Label: *King Louie by Holiday*, aqua shirt jac, with deep aqua, gold, and brown tri-color braid trim on collars and patch pocket, double hem on cuffs. Direct embroidery stitching on back. Spun rayon. c. 1960s. $25-$35.

Label: *King Louie by Holiday, Permanent Press,* light yellow shirt jac, one patch pocket. Bowler embroidery on collar. Back features direct embroidery stitching. Rayon. c. 1960s. $60-$70.

Label: *King Louie by Holiday*, white shirt jac with two front printed panels, concealed pocket on left panel, sewn cuffed sleeves. Embroidered name on back. Rayon. c. 1960s. $35-$45.

Label: *Ten Strike by King Louie*, woman's red cropped shirt, contrasting white shawl collar and front panels, straight hem vented at sides. Embroidered patch on back. Rayon. c. 1940s. $25-$30.

Label: *Ten Strike by King Louie*, rust brown, two button patch pockets, shirttail hem. Direct embroidery stitching on back including the name on the center back yoke. Note that the name has been stitched over the label. Rayon. c. 1940. $60-$70.

Embroidery inside the shirt, shown reverse over label.

Wood and brass trophy, 1956-57.

103

Label: *Ten Strike by King Louie*, pale yellow with dyed to match buttons, two patch pockets with flaps, shirttail hem. No embroidery on shirt. Rayon. c. 1950s. $15-$25.

Ceramic teapot cleverly made with bowling ball and two pins. c. 1960. $30-$40.

Label: *Ten Strike by King Louie*, red, two buttoned patch pockets, buttons dyed to match shirt, shirttail hem. Front patch with Mobil Pegasus is repeated on back. A plastic Pegasus hangs by an elastic cord from a front button. Back has flocked lettering. Rayon. c. 1950s. $75-$100.

Label: *King Louie Ten Strike*, white with contrasting black collar, black buttons, one patch pocket, shirttail hem. Back has pleated side vents that tapered at the waist, an embroidered patch, and direct embroidery stitching. Rayon. c. 1960. $75-$100.

Label: *King Louie Ten Strike*, salmon-colored shirt jac with adjustable button tabs, cuffed sleeves, top stitching on collar. Direct embroidery stitching on front with novelty three crown stitching design, flocked printing on back. The bowler image on the collar was unique to King Louie. Rayon. c. 1950s. $50-$60.

Label: *King Louie Ten Strike*, white with contrasting green collar, green buttons, one patch pocket, straight bottom hem with side vents. Back features a velour flocked logo patch and printing. Rayon. c. 1950s. $35-$45.

Label: *King Louie Ten Strike*, rust brown with two button patch pockets, pleated back vents tapered at waist. Direct embroidery design in back. Rayon. c. 1950s. $60-$70.

Label: *King Louie Ten Strike*, peacock blue, two button patch pockets, shirttail hem. Direct embroidery stitching. Rayon. c. 1960s. $30-$40.

Label: *King Louie Ten Strike*, yellow shirt jac with stitched cuffed sleeves, yellow buttons, one patch pocket with decorative embroidered crown. Three crown embroidery design on front of shirt and bowler embroidery on collar. Back of shirt has flocked print design. Rayon. c. 1960s. $30-$40.

Label: *King Louie Ten Strike*, white with contrasting black collar and buttons, straight bottom hem with side vents. Back has direct looped embroidery design. Rayon. c. 1960s. $30-$40.

Label: *King Louie Ten Strike*, white shirt jac with two printed diagonal stripe panels, concealed pocket in left front panel. Back has gathered back and flocked printing. Rayon. c. 1960s. $40-$50.

Detail of concealed pocket in front panel.

Brass male and female bowler on plastic base, 1954-55.

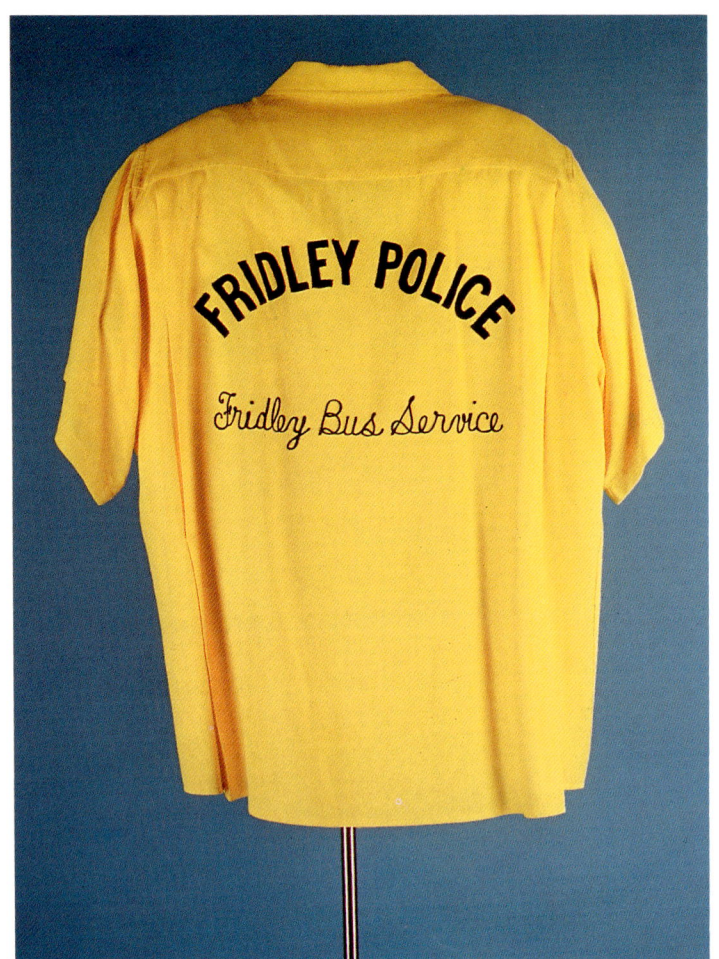

Label: *King Louie Ten Strike*, bright yellow with matching buttons, two button patch pockets, shirttail hem. Direct embroidery crossed pistols over front pocket, lettering in back. Rayon. c. 1960s. $60-$70.

Label: *King Louie Ten Strike*, white with contrasting green collar, one patch pocket, chain stitched embroidery on sleeve, over chest pocket, and on back shoulder, straight bottom hem. Back has direct embroidery stitching. Rayon. c. 1960s. $30-$40.

Label: *King Louie Ten Strike*, orange, two front button patch pockets, slightly tapered at waist, shirttail hem. Direct embroidery tiger design on back. Buttons are dyed to match shirt. Rayon. c. late 1950s. $100-$125.

Label: *King Louie*, green long sleeve shirt with adjustable two button cuffs, two button front pockets, pleated side vents in back tapered at waist, straight hem. Direct embroidery back design. Gabardine. c. 1940s. $75-$95.

Label: *King Louie*, turquoise, two front button patch pocket, bowler embroidery on collar, shirttail hem. Back has flocked printing. Rayon. c. 1960s. $30-$40.

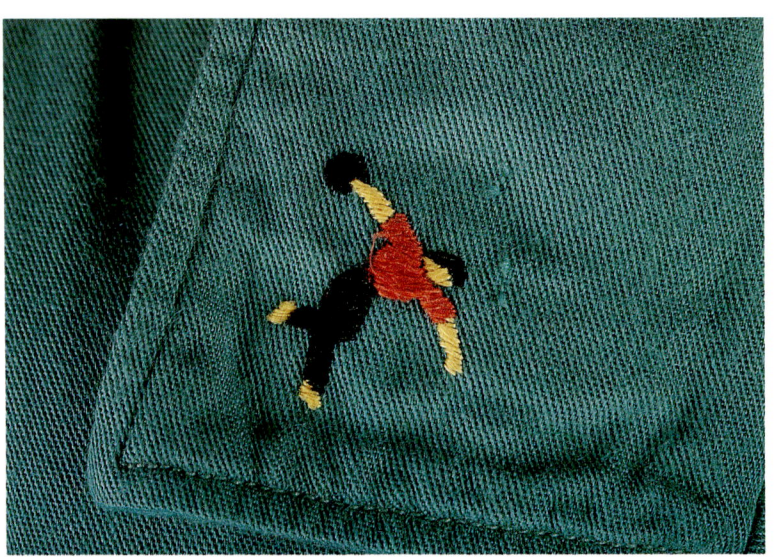

Label: *King Louie*, white with contrasting red collar, one patch pocket with ball and pins embroidery, shirttail hem. Back has contrasting red pleated vents tapered at the waist, and flocked lettering. Rayon. c. 1960s. $30-$40.

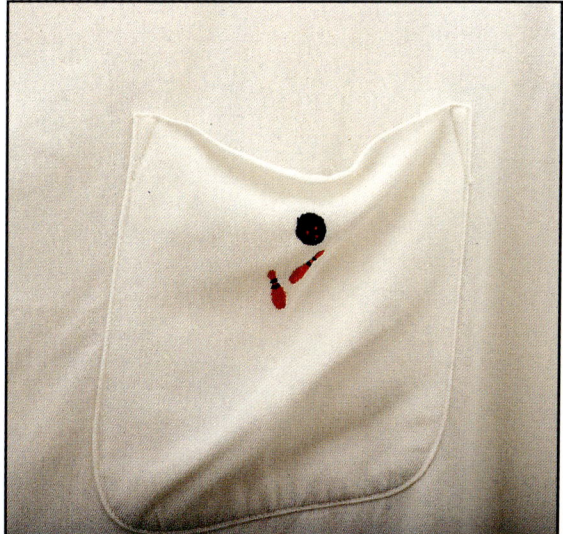

Label: *King Louie - Rite Roll ®* collar, green, concealed buttons under placket front, embroidered tiger on front patch pocket. Direct embroidered back design. Rayon. c. 1960s. $45-$55.

Label: *King Louie by Holiday, Rite Roll ® collar*, gray with pointed collar, two button patch pockets, shirttail hem. Back has vented side pleats tapered at waist, and direct embroidery stitching. Rayon. c. late 1950s or early 1960s. $45-$55.

Label: *King Louie by Holiday - Rite Roll ®* collar, white with two button patch pockets, bowler embroidery on collar, shirttail hem. Back has flocked printed design. Rayon. c. 1950s. $30-$40.

Label: *King Louie Professional Model, Rite Roll ® collar*, mustard gold, concealed buttons under placket front, one patch pocket with embroidered tiger patch, notched sleeves, shirttail hem. Back has embroidered patch and direct embroidery stitching. Rayon flannel. c. 1960s. $50-$60.

Label: *King Louie by Holiday - Rite Roll ® collar*, white with contrasting blue rolled collar, one patch pocket with ball and pins design, bowler embroidery on collar, shirttail hem. Back has contrasting blue pleated side vents tapered at the waist, red flocked printing. Rayon. c. 1960s. $50-$60.

Label: *King Louie, Professional Model*, yellow, one patch pocket with embroidered tiger patch, shirttail hem. Direct embroidery stitching on back. Cotton. c. 1960s. $40-$50.

Label: *King Louie for Junior Bowlers Only, Not Made for Resale*, white with bright blue collar, one patch pocket, shirttail hem. Bowler embroidery on collar. Brunswick logo patch on back. This shirt was a manufacturer's promotional shirt. Rayon. c. 1960s. $30-$40.

Label: *King Louie*, black, contrasting white open collar with embroidered bowler, one patch pocket with embroidered bowling ball and pins, straight bottom hem. Back has contrasting white pleated vents tapered at the waist, and direct embroidery stitching. Rayon. c. 1960s. $40-$50.

Lane Mate

Label: *An Original Lane Mate, All Rayon*, orange with black trim, two front patch pockets, black buttons, straight bottom hem. Front pocket has pins and ball embroidered patch. Back has pleated side vents tapered at waist, and flocked printing. Rayon. c. 1960s. $45-$55.

MacGregor

Label: *MacGregor Frontiers, Made in USA*, army tan, long sleeves with three button cuffs, two front button patch pockets with pointed flaps positioned to the side, placket front. shirttail hem. Back has brown and green direct embroidery stitching. Gabardine. c. 1940s. $65-$75.

Marlboro shirts and sportswear trade show banner or table cloth, handmade of felt. c.1950s or 60s. $50-$75.

Marlboro

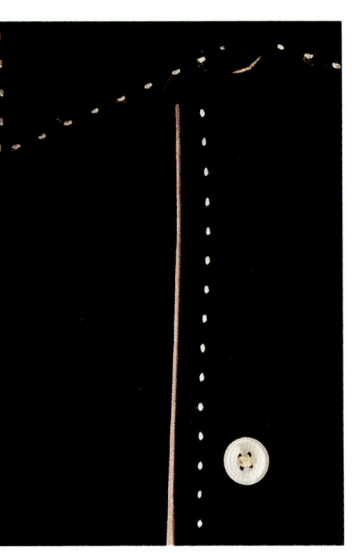

Label: *Marlboro*, dark charcoal gray with contrasting pink top stitching on collar, pockets, and down front of shirt, pink piping trim on front and pockets. Direct embroidery stitching on back. It is unusual that the first and last name are embroidered on back yoke at the shoulders. Rayon. c. 1940s. $100-$125.

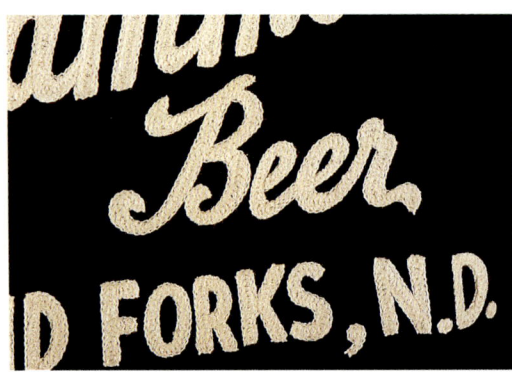

Master Bowler

Label: *Master Bowler*, green long sleeve with button cuffs, two flap pockets, top button loop, shirttail hem, direct embroidery stitching. Rayon. c. 1940s $65-$75.

Label: *Master Bowler*, peacock blue, two front pocket flaps button on the reverse so that button is concealed, shirttail hem. Direct embroidery stitching on back. Rayon. c. 1950s. $30-$40.

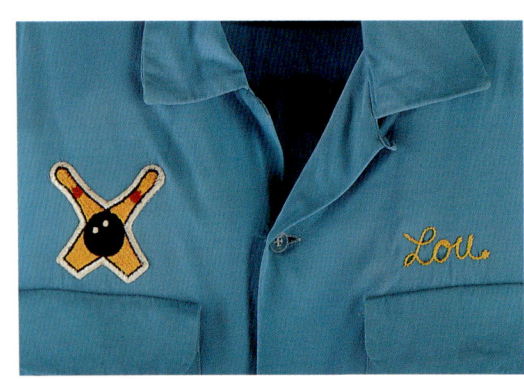

Label: *Master Bowler*, turquoise, two front flap patch pockets with concealed buttons, shirttail hem. Embroidered ball and pins patch over right front pocket. Back has direct embroidery stitching. Rayon. c. 1950s. $75-$100.

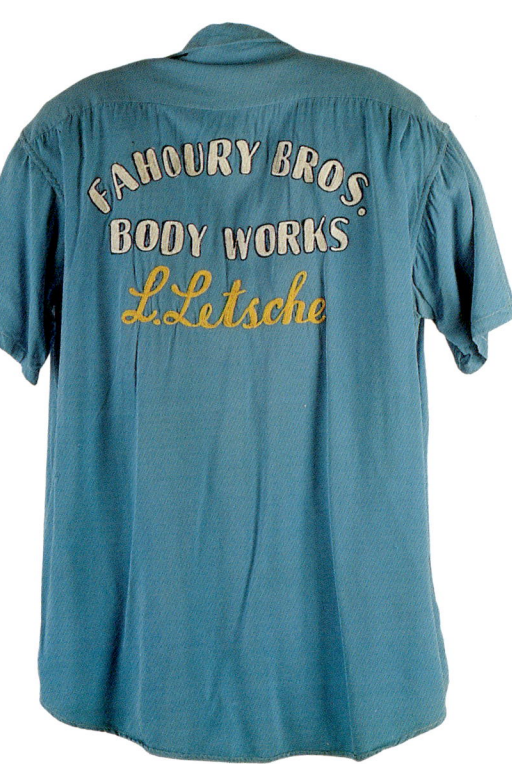

Nat Nast

Label: *Nat Nast*, navy blue with yellow collar and yellow top stitching, two patch pockets with embroidered lion crest, straight hem. Back has contrasting yellow pleated side vents tapered at the waist. Rayon. c. 1960s. $75-$95.

Label: *Nat Nast Creation*, deep aqua, contrasting black collar with aqua top point stitching, double stitched hem on sleeve, two front button pockets with crest patch. Back has two contrasting black peated vents tapered at waist, with flocked printing. Rayon. c. 1960s. $50-$60.

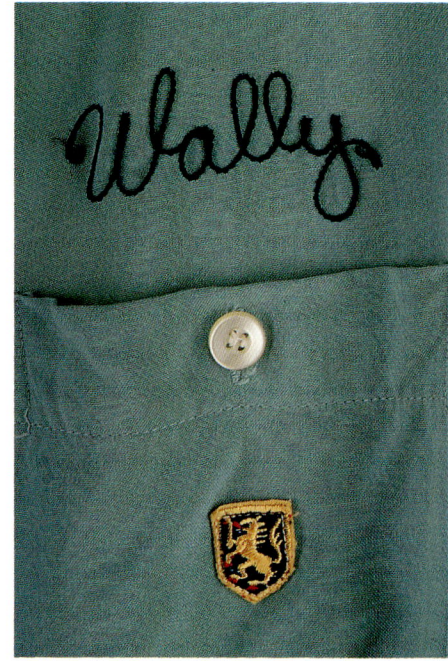

  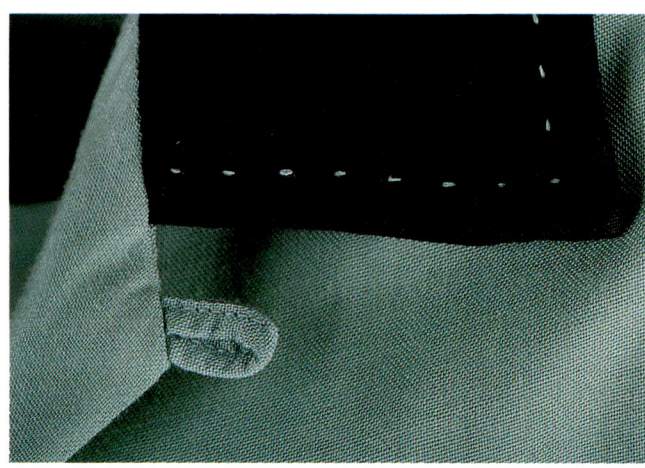

Label: *Nat Nast*, red, one patch pocket with embroidered crown patch, slightly tapered shirt, straight bottom hem. Direct embroidery back design. Cotton-poly blend. c. 1960s. $60-$70.

Label: *Nat Nast Creation*, royal blue with contrasting white collar, white interfacing down front, embroidered felt name patch, two buttom patch pockets, straight bottom hem. Back has contrasting white pleated side vents and white direct embroidery design outlined in red. Rayon. c. 1950s. $75-$95.

Label: *Nat Nast Creation*, yellow with two button patch pointed flap pockets, shirttail hem. Back has pleated side vents tapered at the waist, and direct embroidery stitching. Rayon. c. 1960s. $30-$40.

Label: *Nat Nast Creation*, white with one patch pocket, sewn double cuffed sleeves, straight bottom hem. Back has direct embroidery stitching. Rayon. c. 1960s. $30-$40.

Label: *Nat Nast Creation*, white with contrasting red collar with white top stitching, two button patch pockets, straight bottom hem. Lion crest embroidered patch on front pocket. Back has contrasting red pleated side vents tapered at the waist, and novelty "roadrunner" direct embroidery design. Rayon. c. 1960s. $100-$150.

Label: *Nat Nast Creation*, mint green shirt jac, contrasting black elastic knit waist band on back of shirt, double loop button at neck, novelty trim with bowler and pin on sleeve and on front patch pocket. Direct embroidery stitching on back of shirt. Rayon. c. 1960s. $60-$70.

Novelty trim on sleeve.

Olympian

Label: *Olympian, The Chelsea*, lavender-gray shirt jac with contrasting black braid trim on sleeves and button patch pocket, direct embroidered back design. Note that the buttons down the front of the shirt are placed in twos. Rayon. c. 1950s. $50-$60.

Label: *Olympian, The York*, black with two button patch pockets, straight bottom hem. Back has red direct embroidery stitching. Gabardine. c. 1950s. $50-$60.

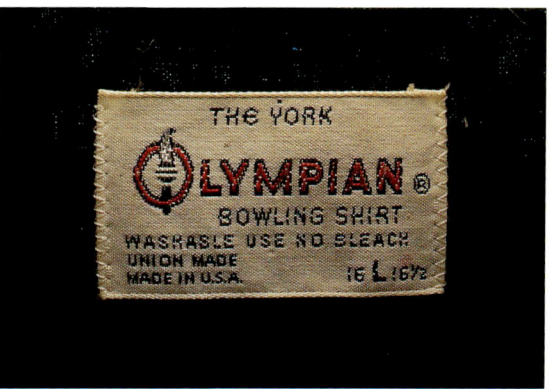

Richman 300

Label: *Richman 300 Brand*, brown, long sleeves with adjustable buttoned cuffs, pointed collar, contrasting top stitching, two front patched pockets with center folded pleats, shirttail hem, direct embroidery on back with red outline, two back pleats. Rayon. c. 1950s. $75-$95.

Sea Island

Label: *Sea Island Extra Long Sleeves and Body*, gray with pointed collars, two front flap patch pockets, long sleeves with adjustable cuffs, top stitching on collar and pocket flaps, straight bottom hem. Back features embroidered *Reddy Killowatt* logo patch. Gabardine. c. 1940s. $100-$125.

Service Bowling Shirt

Label: *Cheswick Service Bowling Shirt*, white with contrasting navy blue collar and front shoulder panels, two front button patch pockets, straight bottom hem. Back has contrasting navy yoke, navy pleated side vents tapered at the waist, and direct embroidery. Rayon. c. 1960s. $35-$45.

Label: *Cheswick Service Bowling Shirt, Union Made*, white with contrasting navy blue collar, two front button patch pockets, shirttail hem. Back features a contrasting navy blue yoke and pleated side vents tapered at waist. Direct embroidery stitching in back. The name embroidery on the right shoulder is rare. Rayon. c. 1960s. $40-$50.

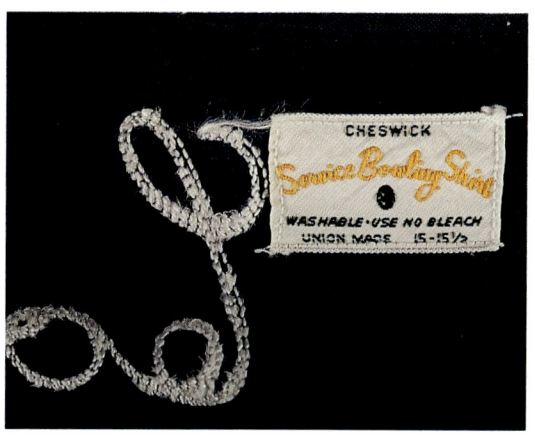

Detail of inside back.

Label: *Fairline Service Bowling Shirt, Union Made*, white, long sleeves with adjustable button cuffs, two button patch pockets with pointed flaps, shirttail hem. Direct embroidery stitching in back. Cotton. c. 1950. $30-$40.

Label: *Major Leaguer Service Bowling Shirt, Union Made*, white, long sleeves with adjustable cuffs, novelty metal buttons with the Shriner's logo, two button pointed flap buttons, shirttail hem. Fancy direct embroidered Shriner's logo on collar and back. Rayon. c. 1950s. $60-$70.

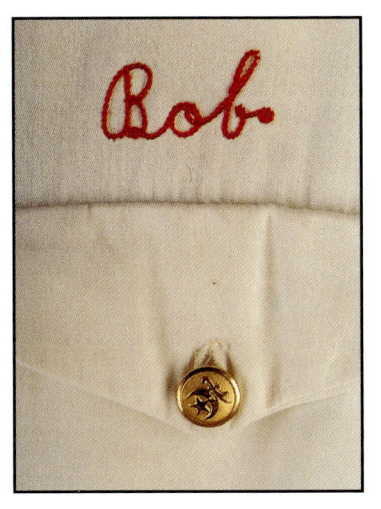

Label: *The Stretch-Jac Service Bowling Shirt*, red shirt jac with black and white ribbing under arms, top button loop, cuffed sleeves, button patched pocket, direct embroidered chained stitching. Spun rayon. c. 1950s. $50-$60.

Shapely Classic

Label: *Shapely Classic, Imported Fabric*, rust red woman's shirt that has been converted into a bowling shirt, wide cuffs with two buttons, rounded collars, patch pocket, straight bottom hem. Direct embroidery stitching. Combed cotton. c.1960s. NPA.

Shorty Bowlaway

Label: *Shorty Bowlaway*, a George London Original, white with two button patch pockets. Back has pleated side vents tapered at waist, and flocked printing. Rayon. c. 1960s. $30–$40.

Smoky Bowling

Label: *Smoky Bowling Shirt (from Nuremberg, Germany)*, light blue with white trim on collar, sleeves and two button patch pockets, white undercollar trim, shirttail hem. Embroidered patch on right shoulder. Back has pleated side vents tapered at waist, and direct embroidery stitching. Combed cotton. c. 1960s. $40-$50.

T. K. Embroidery

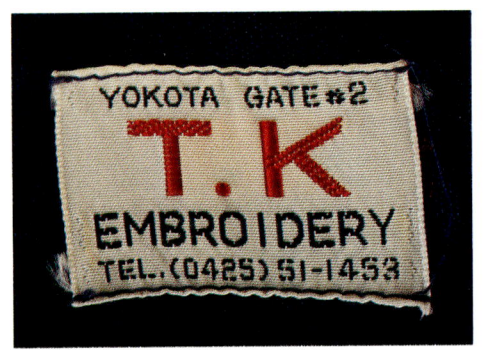

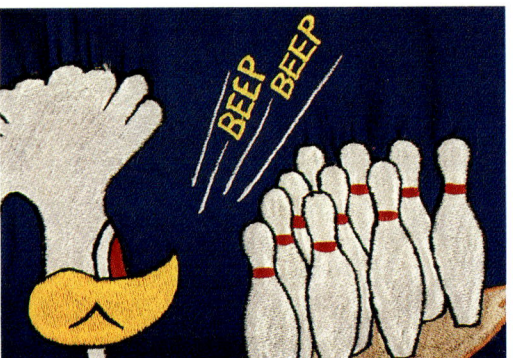

Label: *T. K. Embroidery, Jokota Gate No.2*, woman's shirt, cobalt blue with contrasting light blue trim on sleeves, front patch pocket, and pleated side vents tapered at waist. Direct embroidery roadrunner design on back. Rayon. c. 1950s. $65-$75.

The Lord Penguin

Label: *The Lord Penguin Bowling Shirt by Munsingwear*, cream knit pullover shirt with contrasting black collar, and knit stretch panels under arms, one patch pocket with embroidered penguin logo, straight bottom hem. Back has printed design. Cotton. c. 1960s. $20-$30.

The Strike

Label: *The Strike*, dark navy blue, two front button pointed flaps on pockets, long sleeves with adjustable two button cuffs, straight bottom hem. Back has direct embroidery stitching. Gabardine. c. 1950s. $75-$100.

The Swingster

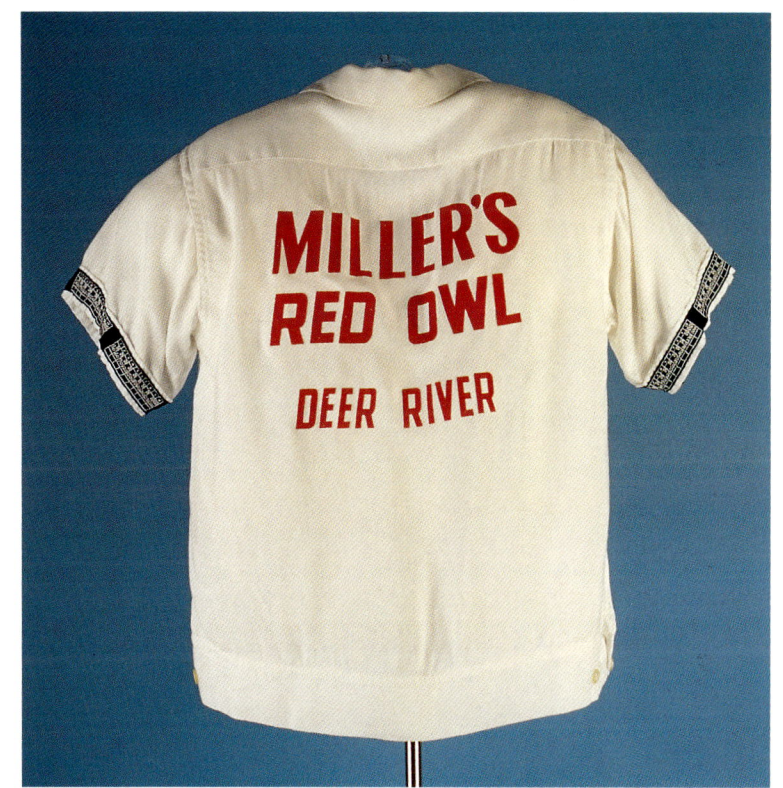

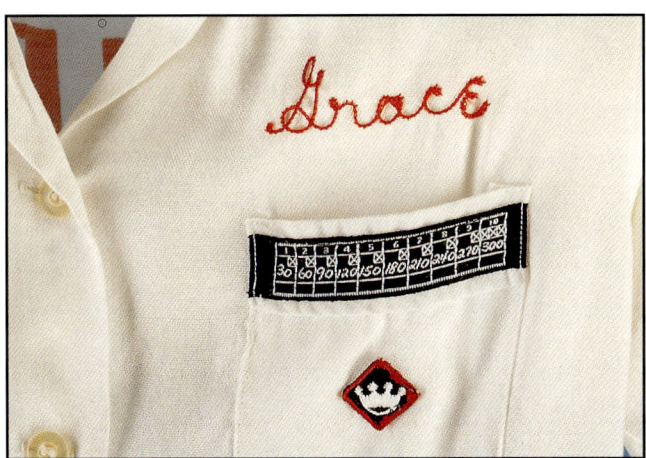

Label: *The Swingster*, white shirt jac with black and white 300 game scorecard novelty trim on patch pocket and on sleeves. Pocket features diamond shape crown embroidered patch. Back has flocked printing. Spun rayon. c. 1960s. $20-$40.

301, Better Than Perfect

Label: *301, Better Than Perfect*, bright peacock blue shirt jac, one patch pocket, direct embroidery name over front pocket and design in back. Rayon. c. 1960. $75-$100.

300 Series

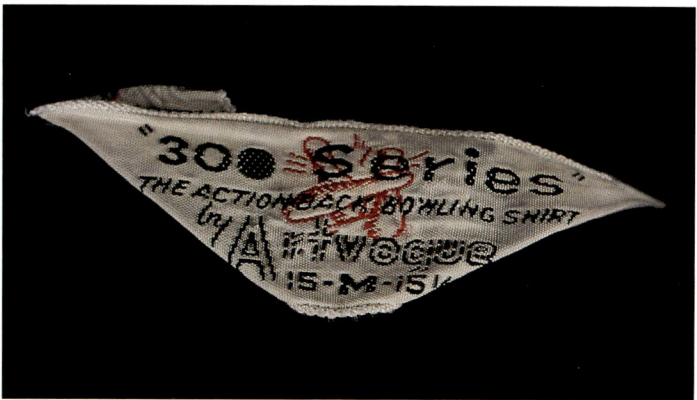

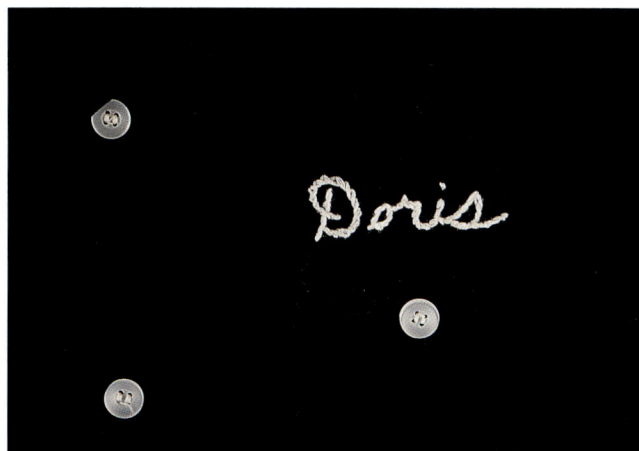

Label: *300 Series, The Action Back Bowling Shirt by Artvogue*, two black shirts (Dick and Doris), each with two front button patch pockets, straight bottom hem. Back has direct embroidery design. It's rare to find two shirts from the same team. Rayon. c. 1960s. $40-$50 each.

Topps

Label: *Topps, Rochester, Indiana*, gray with top button loop, two flap patch pockets, shirttail hem. Back and front has embroidered logo patch. Direct embroidery stitching and patch are backed by cheesecloth. Sanforized cotton. c. 1960s. $75–$85.

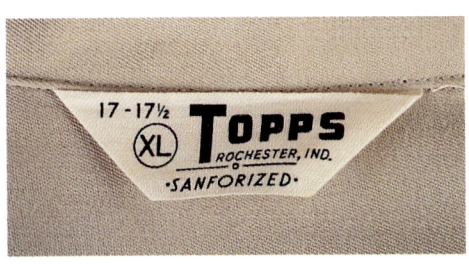

Cheese cloth backing of embroidery and patch, shown on inside back of shirt.

Webber Bowling Shirt Company

Label: *Webber Bowling Shirt Co., Los Angeles,* gray, two front patch pockets with point stitching, long sleeves with cuffs, straight bottom top stitched hem. An interesting feature is the satin back yoke interfacing. Back has direct embroidery stitching. Gabardine. c. 1950s. $50-$60.

Label: missing, pea green, long sleeves with pointed cuffs, two patch pockets with pointed flaps, shirttail hem. Back has embroidered patch lettering and embroidered design. Rayon. c. early 1950s. $60-$70.